THE RUSSELL LUPIN STORY

Pat Edwards

The portrait by Jane Bown that appeared in The Observer *on the occasion of George Russell receiving the MBE in 1950, the year before he died at the age of 94.*

ABOUT THE N.C.C.P.G.

The National Council for the Conservation of Plants and Gardens was formed in 1978, because a number of people realised that with the commercial pressures that Nurseries, Garden Centres, etc. were under many old and cultivated varieties of plants were being lost for ever. As they were the result of many generations of Gardeners, Hybridists and Nurserymen, mostly from Britain, devoting huge amounts of time and effort, this is a great shame.

What followed was the creation of National Plant Collections®. These are collections of families of plants that are taken care of by a varied selection of people. They may be keen individuals, or institutions like the National Trust or Botanic Gardens. Collection Holders become expert in their own family of plants and have agreed to keep records and share their knowledge and expertise, even sharing propagation material, to ensure that the many types of plants are saved from extinction.

There are now nearly 700 National Collections, and they all need support and monitoring, to make sure they are up to a national standard. A small staff at Headquarters carries out this work. With the technical advance of computers it was realized that the experience and in some cases almost legendary information should be held on a database. The Demeter Project was launched, and in 2002 received funding from the Lottery Fund.

From small beginnings has grown this organization, now beginning to spread internationally. There is now a Web Site at www.nccpg.com where information about the activities of the 42 regional groups can be accessed.

If you are interested in saving our garden plants we hope you will join the NCCPG – apply on-line or telephone (01483)211465 for an application form.

CONTENTS

ACKNOWLEDGEMENTS

I would like to express my thanks to the many people who have helped me with this project. Firstly on the practical side Tom Reeves, who kept the Russell strain alive in the dark days when the old nursery was fading. Arthur Heard, who spared time to teach me so much of what George Russell had taught him. More recently thanks to John Massey and his team for their huge enthusiasm and backing.

Help with the publication has been gratefully received, Elspeth Napier has proof-read my copy, and given me so much valuable advice on the technicalities of writing the booklet.

The staff at the Printers, Livesey Limited, have been most patient and kind with the scanning and layout of the old pictures. The pictures on pages 24, 25, 37, 38, 39 plus the back cover were taken by John Glover, who came to Albrighton especially, for which many thanks.

Chapter 1

GEORGE RUSSELL

George Russell was born in 1857, in the village of Stillington, about 10 miles north of York, where his father was a cobbler.

Life in a Yorkshire village then would have been quite peaceful and settled. The Crimean conflict, with Britain and France at war with Russia, had just ended. The Great Exhibition of 1851 at Hyde Park in London, had confirmed the superiority of British industry, and the Empire overseas, with access to the raw materials to feed that industry, was becoming well established, in spite of setbacks like the Indian Mutiny having to be quelled.

Although by today's standards the folk who worked in factories or mines did so in appalling conditions, an established cobbler would have made a comfortable living, and be able to provide a stable home and an adequate education for the young George, which was evident in his caring attitude and obvious intelligence in later life. He always rose at 5am, and read two newspapers before going to work, so he would have been very much in touch with the developments of the day, no doubt reading with interest articles about such things as Mendel's experiments with the genetics of peas, published in English in 1901, or the introduction of new plants from far away places.

George Russell with the young boy Arthur (Sonny) Heard in Yorkshire.

There was a great interest in horticulture in Victorian times. New species of trees and shrubs were coming in, particularly from America and Asia. The great landowners of the day competed with each other to grow the novelties, and the burgeoning middle classes were beginning to be actively involved with growing both vegetables for the house and ornamental flowers in their gardens. The Royal Horticultural Society, which had been founded in 1804, encouraged the enthusiasm for new introductions and described methods of growing all kinds of exotic fruits vegetables and plants. The magazine *The Gardener's Chronicle* was very popular, and was a means of disseminating information to a wider public. Most villages had their Garden Society, and one of George Russell's earliest memories was of being taken along to a local flower show.

As a young man George Russell worked for Backhouse Nursery in York. This was a thriving business at that time, with more than 100 acres of land near York, specialising in tropical plants, alpines, fruit trees and hardy plants of all kinds. At some stage he also worked for Pennells of Lincoln, another well-known nursery firm. This background of solid commercial experience would have given him a very sound knowledge of the properties that denoted a good plant.

An early picture of George Russell on his allotment near York.

No doubt George Russell would have continued working as a nurseryman, but, having married, and set up home in Kensington Street, York, where he and his wife had a son, his wife became ill. In order to look after her he turned to jobbing gardening, probably earning about 10 shillings for a full day. This involved working for a number of different employers in the area. This flexible arrangement enabled him to nurse his wife, which he did most devotedly until she died.

George Russell outside his cottage at Copmanthorpe, near York.

When he lost his wife a kindly neighbour, Mrs. Heard, looked after the widower. She had a young son, Arthur, who became ill. Fresh air was prescribed, and so George Russell would take the youngster, who he always called Sonny, with him on his gardening jobs, and to work on his allotment.

The allotment had provided a site for the growing of fruit and vegetables, and here he had also tried out some hybridizing of various flowers, including daffodils and aquilegias. Aquilegias or columbines, sometimes also known as Granny's Bonnets, have a wide range of colours. Various species of aquilegias, that is the different members of the genus or family that can breed together, included flowers of each primary colour. pure red, yellow and blue are present in different members of the family so that, potentially, all the colours of the rainbow are possible if these species are crossed to produce progeny with a mixture of the primary colours in their inherited characteristics. Aquilegias are very pretty, but the colours are fairly muted, giving a pastel, fairy-like effect. Maybe it was these early

The cottage has not changed much to this day; this photograph was taken in 2003.

George Russell's allotments are also still there in Bishopthorpe. The Terry chocolate factory can be seen beyond, with York racecourse on the left.

Eventually George Russell needed two allotments, he is pictured here on the allotments with the lupins.

experiments that pointed the way towards the lupins, which also have the full range of colour in their genes, but in much more vivid tones.

In 1911, when George Russell was aged 54, one of his employers, a Mrs. Micklethwaite, had arranged a vase of lupins, which caught his eye. Very probably these were the Californian perennial lupin, *Lupinus polyphyllus*, which was introduced into this country in 1826. It is blue - purple in the wild, but can produce blooms of reddish purple, or sometimes white, and is a stately plant 3 - 6 feet in height. The catalogue for Baker's Nurseries of Wolverhampton in 1909 lists plants of this "Old fashioned Garden Lupin" at 6d each, albus (white), roseus (pink) as well as the novelty, *Lupinus polyphyllus Moe*rheims. This was described as "one of the finest herbaceous plants ever sent out, with fine long spikes of rose and white coloured flowers". It sold at the princely sum of 2 shillings each, worth 1/5th of a day of George Russell's work!

The flower spikes of these *Lupinus polyphyllus* and its hybrids would have been fairly lax, with spaces between the individual blossoms. Mrs. Micklethwaite's flower arrangement is reputed to have sparked off the resolution to try to "improve" the garden lupin in George Russell's mind. Whether he consciously felt he could better the form of the plant and bloom as well as the colour of course we do not know, but he maintained that he always knew what he was aiming for.

Chapter 2

THE LUPINS

The name Lupinus derives from the Latin lupus, meaning wolf. The reason for this was that the plant was seen to be greedy, in that it smothered out other plants. Later, the deep rooting characteristics of the plants were deemed to impoverish the soil. In fact the opposite is true, as the plant belongs to the family Leguminaceae, which grow nodules on their roots, which release nitrogen into the soil, thus enriching it.

Early in the 20th century work had been done by the well-known nurseryman James Kelway, crossing *Lupinus polyphylla* with the tree lupin, *Lupinus arboreus*. This species has fragrant yellow or blue flowers on a shrubby plant, which is questionably hardy in an area such as Yorkshire, and bears branches of short spikes. This was followed by work on similar lines by G.R. Downer and John Harkness. It is probable that George Russell knew about, and may have managed to obtain some of these new strains. Also available at the time were *Lupinus polyphllus* varieties *argenteus, flexuosus, laxiflorus, Lachmanni, rivularis* and *grandiflorus*, all from North America. These were listed in William Robinson's book *The English Flower Garden*, of 1903, so would have definitely been familiar, at least by name, to George Russell in 1911.

Also listed in this publication was *Lupinus nootkatensis*, a dwarfed species from N.W. America, which continued in bloom for a long time, and a number of annual types in a variety of colours. The book notes that as they grow quickly, they need not be sown until mid April, and will thrive on any common soil. These annuals included L. *sub-carnosus*, a beautiful ultramarine blue and *L. hybridus atrococcineus*, the finest of all, having long graceful spikes of a bright crimson scarlet, with white tips. Other excellent types recommended were *L. mutabilis, L. crukshanksii, L. Menziesii, L.luteus, L superbus, L. pubescens, L. Hartwegii,* and the varieties of *L. Dunnettii*. Mr. Robinson commented that 'The many sorts were so much alike that they were not worth separating, but that 'the smaller annual lupins are very pretty, and could be charmingly used to precede late blooming and taller plants'.

There were a surprising number of seed varieties generally available at that time. Besides the *Lupinus polyphyllus* types, the perennial seed selection in Baker's catalogue of 1909 listed the fragrant yellow tree lupin, *Lupinus arboreus lutea*, and a white variety of it known as 'Snow Queen' was offered as a plant. In addition the seed selection listed hardy annual lupins at 3d per packet as follows:
'*L. albo-coccineus nanus*. (From the Levant) 1 ft. The lower half of the flower is of a rich rosy crimson, the upper half pure white.
L. cruckshanksii. (From the Peruvian Andies) 3 ft. Dark blue and white flowers.

A very old slide of George Russell, about 1937, with the lupin that was named for him.

A Baker's Nursery catalogue from 1937, the year that Russell Lupin strain was introduced to great worldwide acclaim.

Arthur 'Sonny' Heard (1937).

Lupins make very attractive cut flowers.

The huge Shire horses continued to hoe between the lupins until the end of the 1950s. They rarely damaged the crop.

L. Hartwegii. (From Mexico) 2 ft. A real royal blue, standards prettily marked white. Var. *caelestinus*, lovely light blue, quite a distinct shade, greatly admired in the trials at our nurseries.
L. hybridus atrococcineus. (A hybrid) 2½ft. Large spikes of scarlet white tipped flowers, very effective.
L. mutabilis roseus. (From South America) Beautiful rose, standards when open blotched yellow, gradually turning to apricot. Quite a new and distinct shade.
L. nanus. (From California) 1 ft. Blue and white. Var albus. White.
L. sulphureus superbus. 2 ft. Beautiful old gold, sometimes tinged bronze.'
Also listed was Lupin seed in Rose, White, Yellow and Blue, all hardy annuals, 2½ft.

It can be noted here that the primary colours of red and blue were well represented among the lupin family at the beginning of the century. The missing ingredient was yellow, which was available in the tree lupin, *Lupinus arboreus*, which was not ideal from the point of view of a fine herbaceous plant, and in the European *Lupinus luteus*, which unfortunately was an annual species.

The resolution to 'improve' the *Lupinus polyphyllus* led to George Russell considering his ideal plant. This ideal would be a compact, disease free plant, truly perennial, that is, would continue to flower year after year. It would include all the colours of the rainbow, thus providing garden artists with a complete palette of hues. The spike would be solid with florets from near the ground to the top, not showing any of the stem between them. This implied that the shape of each floret would be enlarged, having a large, fat 'bell', or keel, and also that the standards, or petals that stand up at the back of the keel, should hold themselves straight up, in other words would not lean backwards, producing a 'pinched' effect, nor fold forward, making the floret look 'hooded'. It would be sturdy enough not to need staking, and, if the flower heads were removed, thus preventing it from producing seed, it would continue to flower through the summer and into the autumn.

To achieve these objectives he set about obtaining seed of any species of lupin that he felt had the characteristics that his paragon should include.

There is no record of exactly where George Russell obtained his seed, although it seems certain that he did write off to sources in Europe, maybe for the 1-1½ ft *Lupinus luteus*, a hardy annual which grows in southern Europe, bright yellow, with a lovely scent, which had been introduced to Britain as early as 1590. He probably would also have used the annual 'Texas Bluebonnet', *Lupinus subcarnosus*, a beautiful ultramarine shade with white or cream on the standard, from North America. Experts in the 1930's guessed that he used *Lupinus laxifolius*, and *Lupinus lepidus* from high in Oregon, with blue flowers and silvered leaves. *Lupinus leucophyllus* and *Lupinus nootkatensis*, a short lived perennial with blue florets tipped with red or yellow and about 3 ft in height from Alaska were also quoted as possibilities.

The seedlings of species that are grown in isolation, and so cannot cross with another species usually turn out to be similar to the parent. When two species are cross-pollinated, to produce a hybrid, the result can be any mix of the thousands of characteristics of both parents.

George Russell's allotments were gradually were taken over by lupin seedlings and he needed to acquire a second one. At first he grew from his bought seed packets, then he sowed the seeds from the best. Once these were mature, and flowers were being produced, he started to take the seeds from them. He always maintained that he never actually 'crossed' the flowers artificially, as most modern hybridists do.

George Russell just allowed his flowers to be pollinated in the normal way, which is by bumblebees. They are heavy enough to weigh down the 'keel', or 'bell, of the flower when they land upon it to take nectar or pollen. The stamens with their pollen, and the stigma, which is the sticky receiving organ leading to the ovary, where the seed is formed, then jump up and rub against the bumblebee's furry bottom. The pollen thus collected on the bee then gets transferred to the next flower, ensuring cross-pollination.

He must have grown hundreds of seedlings from the seeds that resulted from the cross-pollination of his original pure native species and the hybrids or mixed types that he bought from various nurserymen who had already tried their hands at hybridizing the Lupins. As they matured he examined each plant and spike of flowers with his very discerning and critical eye, and discarded all the ones that did not satisfy him, probably a very large proportion.

In this way, with incredible patience, and over the next quarter of a century, George Russell's allotments very gradually became home to a new and beautiful strain of lupins. The form of the plants altered to become a strong and compact shape. The spikes of blossom stood up to the weather, clothed from top to bottom in a solid mass of florets. Most amazing were the colours, a whole rainbow of hues, some bi-coloured, or two colours on one floret, usually the bell being one colour and the standard another. Others were 'selfs', or all of the blossoms the same. Some were shaded with the florets grading from a light colour as they came out, becoming darker as they matured.

They were such a brilliant show that gardeners began to notice them, word was passed around, and people began to come to see and admire the wonderful spectacle of these marvelous blooms.

Nurserymen could also see that there were commercial prospects allied to these flowers, and George Russell found himself being offered large sums of money for individual plants or the right to propagate them. £5 for a thimbleful of seed from an enthusiastic American, or £50 for a single plant. All these offers were turned down. The old man was not interested in money; he felt he had enough for his needs. He told people that they could look, but not buy. Also, that he had not yet completed the job of 'improving' the lupins.

George Russell pictured working among the lupins with the 'boy' Arthur (Sonny) Heard.

Chapter 3

JAMES BAKER

In the village of Codsall, near Wolverhampton, there was an extraordinary nurseryman called James Baker. His father had been a successful businessman connected with the shoe trade in the town who set up his two sons, James and Norman, with some land at Codsall. Norman ran a successful landscape business, many gardens around Wolverhampton were laid out in the 'Baker's of Codsall' style, usually with the hallmark of Harold Mills, the landscape director stamped upon them. Typically they incorporated rock and water features, and were planted up with a range of trees, shrubs, herbaceous plants and alpines all supplied from the Nursery.

James Baker, the owner of Baker's Nursery, who was reputed to be able to recognise a good plant or a good footballer when he saw one!

James Baker ran the nursery side of the business. He was a shrewd businessman, who had a remarkable eye for a good plant. Apparently he could spot a good footballer as well, he was chairman of the Wolverhampton Wanderers football club at the time when they won the FA Cup and the League Championship on several occasions, with such famous names as Billy Wright and Ron Flowers in the team, and Stan Cullis as the manager. However, that is another story; at the nursery Jimmy Baker introduced a host of wonderful plants to the public. Symons Jeune phlox, Ballard michaelmas daisies, Otley Korean chrysanthemums and Bishop delphiniums were all famous. The nursery was well known the world over for the quality and variety of its plants, especially the herbaceous perennials.

When the plants were in flower the nursery was a picture, great blocks of colour from the plants in the fields, where Shire horses still pulled the ploughs or harrows between the plants. Labour was cheap at that time, there could be a queue of men at the gate waiting to be taken on, so any slackers risked being quickly given their 'cards' by the foreman, Mr Moody, if their work was not satisfactory, and another would be employed. The work was hard and often monotonous, as all the plants that the horses could not get through were hoed throughout the summer, and 'turned in', i.e. the soil turned over with a spade, during the winter. Another Mr Mills ran the dispatch sheds and warehouses, where thousands of plants would be sent out every year by post or rail, beautifully packed, having been ordered from the catalogues which were sent out at least twice annually. Mr Mills also took fantastic exhibitions to flower shows all over the country, such as Southport, Shrewsbury and Handsworth, culminating in the biggest one, at Chelsea in London. At these shows more orders would be taken, to be dispatched at 'Lifting Time', starting about the third week in October. This meant an extremely busy time from October to Christmas, when the weather could become hard, and plants could not be dispatched any more.

George Russell was featured on the front cover of Baker's catalogue in 1938, wearing his familiar 'granddad' shirt, with no collar.

Jimmy Baker heard about the amazing show of lupins on the allotments in York, he also must have heard about George Russell's reluctance to sell his wonderful plants. He went to see the old man in 1935 and admired the plants, but it seems that he did not mention money at all. He took quite another tack, telling him that it was selfish to keep the fantastic plants to himself. He persuaded George Russell that he should give the public a chance to see and grow his magnificent blooms. He offered to take over all the propagation and promotion of the strain, and give him the chance to tranquilly concentrate on his selecting and rogueing out for the rest of his life, with no worries about money matters. After thinking about it for three days George Russell agreed to James Baker's proposals. It was agreed that the strain should always be known as the Russell Lupin, and also that 'Sonny' Heard should go to the Nursery with the plants, thus ensuring that he would have a job and carry on the Russell methods.

So it was arranged, the plants were marked and moved to Boningale that autumn. The next year, 1936, a house was organized for him on the new Nursery at Boningale, a 30 acre site that had recently been added to the Nurseries at Codsall, about 3 miles away. Arthur ("Sonny") Heard and his new wife, Betty, agreed to go with him and look after his needs. Arthur Heard would be his assistant, and would be taught all the techniques that George Russell had developed, so that there would be a continuation of the knowledge and experience of the last quarter of a century.

George Russell had never actually propagated any of his own hybrids at all; he had just concentrated on growing new seedlings and eliminating all the inferior ones, very gradually improving the strain. The 1,500 plants, all of them different, were taken from the York allotment to be planted at Boningale, and all the best were propagated by cuttings and planted out. The first work that George Russell and his assistant

The scene at Boningale in 1938, when the bank was a glorious mass of colour, 80,000 people came to view the blossoms.

undertook was to select and rogue the seedlings that had been planted out. To the horror of the staff and James Baker they cast out 4,800 of the 5,000 plants, leaving only 200 in the first year.

Of these certain selections were to be launched to the public as named hybrids in 1938. On June 8th 1937 the first major exhibition of seedlings was staged in copper bowls at the R.H.S. Flower Show in London, and won the coveted R.H.S. Gold medal, and later the Williams Memorial Medal for the best exhibit of the year made 'of one genus showing excellence in cultivation'. It covered 500 square feet, and caused a furore, not only in horticultural circles, but also in the international press. Never before, or probably since, has the introduction of a new strain of plants made such a hit with the public. The radiant colours and the vastly improved form of the lowly lupin merited all the accolades that were heaped upon George Russell, and the romantic story of an old man spending his twilight years on the patient selection without thought of reward appealed to all. Suddenly, at the age of 80, George Russell became world famous. *Horticultural Trade World*, New York, headlined 'Super Lupines, Wonder Work of an Octogenarian'. *The Manchester Guardian* hailed 'A new Race of Lupins'. The *Ottawa Journal* called them the 'most spectacular flowers of many years' and the *Sydney Mail* said 'George Russell's Triumph has been hailed in all parts of the World'. The Madison Cooper's gardening magazine, New York called them a 'Floral sensation', while the *Evening Citizen*, Ottawa wrote about 'Luxuriant Lupins produced by veteran English grower'

The Nursery at Boningale is situated on a bank, which faces to the south, and in 1937 the whole area was massed with lupins, in rows and blocks. 80,000 people

George Russell showing visitors the lupins at Boningale.

The old man surrounded by admirers.

People crowded to see the lupins in flower during June.

The lupin seeds were considered so valuable that they were kept in a bank vault!

The glorious show of lupins caused traffic jams on the Boningale road!

George Russell was kept busy showing people the lupins.

came during June to view the blossoms, which were a truly extraordinary sight. The Nursery charged 6 pence per head, which was donated to the Blind Institute in Wolverhampton. The scores of shades and colours were truly amazing, including self-colours of pink, orange yellow and strawberry red. Bicolours of royal purple and gold, apricot and sky blue, rose pink and amethyst with dozens of intermediate shades and combinations on hundreds of massive spikes filled the bank with radiant colour.

In January 1938 Baker's offered mixed hybrids for sale at 15 shillings per dozen, or 100 plants at 5-10 shillings per dozen. Seed was available, priced at 1 shilling for 12 seeds, (or 1 penny each!) or 10 shillings for 250 seeds. The seeds were considered so valuable that at one time sacks of lupin seed were actually stored in the bank for safekeeping! The Baker's catalogue of autumn 1938 introduced 31 named hybrids for sale, at prices ranging from 5 shillings to 21 shillings each. By 1939 33 more hybrids were introduced, accompanied in the special catalogue by photographs of 25 of the spikes in full colour. Some of the names were obviously chosen by George Russell himself, with connections with his native city of York, in fact one was called 'City of York', then there was 'Catharine of York', and 'Betty of York', as well as 'Mrs. Micklethwaite', after George Russell's past employer who had inspired him with her flower arrangement. There were a series of Boningale varieties, such as 'Boningale Lad', 'Boningale Charm', and 'Boningale Maid'. Jimmy Baker, always ready for a spot of publicity, named many of the hybrids after famous people, who were flattered and pleased to help out with a special launch. Gladys Cooper and both Elsie and Doris Waters came into this category.

Recently I had a telephone call from a Mrs. Jan Kuipers, who was looking for a plant of the Russell Lupin Mrs. Noel Terry to give to her mother, Mrs. Betty Lawrie, the daughter of the original 'Mrs. Noel Terry' whose name was Kathleen. I was not able to supply the plant, but was able to give her a photograph. She told me that her mother is still alive, and delighted to write down her memories of George Russell. This is what she wrote:

"Many famous people have resided around York but few have received more widespread acclaim than George Russell. Mr. Noel Terry, in his late thirties a Managing Director of Joseph Terry & Sons and a well-known freeman of the City of York, often walked from his home bordering Knavesmire to his office at the chocolate factory on the Bishopthorpe Road. Further along the road lay the allotments, two of which were cultivated by George Russell, so it was not surprising that the two men should meet as they knew each other well by sight. Mr. Russell was a small, elderly, slightly bent man with snow white hair and moustache and on one occasion he asked Mr. Terry if he might name his latest hybrid lupin after his wife, Mrs. Noel Terry. His request was willingly granted but after a hard day at the office Mr. Terry completely forgot about the encounter so it was not until the following year, when he was

After George Russell's death in 1951 Baker's Nursery continued to introduce more of his hybrids. This catalogue of 1953 depicts him holding a bunch of his lupins.

The lupin field continued to attract crowds of visitors at lupin time.

Tom Reeves, the herbaceous foreman at Baker's Nursery, who did so much to keep the lupins after George Russell died in 1951.

Mrs Noel Terry herself, pictured in the 1930s.

The original hybrid lupin Mrs Noel Terry *(below left) survived to become part of Pat Edwards' National Collection of Russell Hybrids, but many of the old varieties were diseased or misnamed. The hybrid* Loveliness *still survives in the collection. This is amazing, as it has been propagated by cuttings for over 60 years.*

The colourful crop of seedlings grown at Ashwood Nursery in 2003, showing a far better range of goo

lants than the ones that Pat Edwards grew in 1988, a result of continual selection of the best seedlings.

Pat Edwards' selection in the 1990s, with granddaughter Charlotte skipping through them.

Merlin, to be introduced in 2004.

Above: The scent of lupins is a nostalgic memory for many people, children can smell them much better than adults. Maybe my granddaughter, Victoria, will remember the perfume when she is grown up.

Below: A border in John Massey's garden shows how well lupins look when mixed wth other herbaceous plants.

thumbing the pages of a horticultural catalogue and exclaimed to his wife that she had gone up in price that she discovered how she had been recognized. However, when she saw the plant she was a little disappointed as it was, at her description a "pale, wishy washy pink" and not very outstanding.

Older generations of Yorkshire people will remember the wonderful annual display of lupins that George Russell produced at the York Gala when they would make a beeline for the floral display marquee in order to see what new colour he had achieved for that year. Unlike the other stall holders, when the three days was ended Russell made sure that every lupin stem was carefully removed and put into bags so that no one could obtain so much as a single seed! It was rumoured when he died that he had not passed on the secret of his success even to his son."

George Russell received the Veitch Memorial Medal from the Royal Horticultural Society, a high honour for his work with the lupins. Bakers Nursery was also awarded the coveted Gold Medal and the Williams Memorial Medal for the exhibition at the London show in 1938.

Chapter 4

THE WAR YEARS AND AFTER

So the lupins were off to a good start, Jimmy Baker had kept to his side of the bargain, and done everything possible to make the marvellous flowers available to the general public. But, as we all know now, tragedy was brewing. On September 3rd 1939 war was declared between Britain and Germany. By November of the same year the story was very different. A special catalogue was printed which announced a clearance sale 'To release land for food production. 100,000 Bush and Standard Roses, 50,000 Shrubs and Trees, 200,000 Hedging Plants and an Enormous Quantity of Russell Lupins' were offered at 20% discount. 'Owing to depletion of staff no correspondence can be entered into regarding this offer.' By 1940 a very scaled down leaflet, with no colour, was printed, but of course the excitement had gone from the venture. For the next 5 years the catalogues emphasised 'Vegetables of National Importance'.

However, a war did not stop George Russell, who carried on with his selecting, albeit on a smaller scale. In 1944, when maybe peace was a faint hope, Baker's printed a photograph of the old man on the front of the catalogue, with a vase of his flowers. They informed the public that 'In spite of shortage of staff and the prior claims of food production the roguing and selection of the Russell Lupins is being carried out with conscientious care. Seed of the re-selected stock continues to improve year by year and we look forward to offering an outstanding range of new varieties when normal times return. The many admirers of Mr Russell will be glad to know that although approaching his 90th year, he continues to take a very live interest in everything connected with the garden and his Lupins in particular'.

George Russell at 90 years of age. During the war years the old man continued to select and care for the lupins at Boningale, producing more beautiful hybrids for Baker's to introduce to the public.

After the war the Lupins continued to be selected and rogued by George Russell and his assistant, Arthur Heard. In June of each year the visitors continued to view the lupins at Boningale, often over 20,000 people in a weekend, donating 6d each to the Blind Institute in Wolverhampton. A dwarf tribe of lupins was being selected, which fitted the bill nicely for the smaller, self-maintained gardens that were the vogue in the 50's. By then there were

A tribute to a great gardener

IT is difficult even now to realise that George Russell is no longer with us as it is impossible to pass through the Lupin fields without feeling he isn't far away.

The many letters received at the time of his death suggested a personal loss and this is understandable as this very kindly old gentleman represented the best in the gardening world. He loved every type of flower and at the end was happy in the knowledge that he had done more than his share to bring additional colour and gaiety into many thousands of gardens all over the land.

Although deeply touched when he received the M.B.E. this public recognition of his work and the other honours that came his way made no difference to the man and he remained to the end the same simple unassuming character who asked for nothing more than his work should bring pleasure to others.

Evidence of the esteem in which Mr. Russell was held throughout the country appeared in numerous press notices and we think it fitting that extracts from some of these should be reprinted here.

" Through the lifelong toil of an obscure country labourer, the Russell Lupin is one of the chief glories of the English Garden.

It would be a grand thing to say, of anyone, that they had turned some of the weeds of life into flowers."

Rev. Frank Martin.
Sunday Graphic.

" A simple man of the earth who became world famous as the Lupin man."

Birmingham Despatch.

" A statesman might well envy a man who could be so sure his good work would grow on after him."

The Times.

" Such tributes as paid by a famous Dutch grower: ' You make our tulip fields look drab, Mr. Russell '."

Daily Herald.

" Russell has the finest memorial any man can have—the tall graceful flower he created."

Daily Graphic.

" Year in and year out he showed a remarkable singleness of purpose with the wonderful results we all know."

Smallholder.

" George Russell released into the floral world rays of beauty in a new form and thus gladdened many hearts and strengthened many souls in a time when we so sadly need peace."

Wolverhampton Express and Star.

" He devoted a great part of his life to raising the lupin—to world fame as a flower of unsurpassed beauty with a wide range of varieties."

Birmingham Post.

" As sure of his own niche as Frau Karl Druschki or Mrs. Sinkins is George Russell of Lupin fame."

Liverpool Daily Post.

" Fame comes to people in various ways and gardeners seldom seem to share in it but Geo. Russell . . . certainly was an exception."

Yorkshire Observer.

HE SOUGHT NOT WEALTH OR HIGH RENOWN—
TO SCHOLARSHIP HE LAID NO CLAIM,
AND YET, SO LONG AS FLOWERS ARE GROWN
THE WORLD WILL BLESS GEORGE RUSSELL'S NAME.

C. H. TANDY.

plenty of good selections in the pipeline, and the trade in named hybrids, seedlings and seed continued. In 1946 12 more hybrids were introduced. Competitions were organised for customers to find good hybrids amongst their own seedlings, with £100 prizes, resulting in more good ones being discovered. Baker's Nursery regained its pre-war reputation, and continued to excel at shows and as a mail order business for a number of years, after the war 76 more new hybrids appeared. The Herbaceous Foreman, Tom Reeves, who had worked for Baker's for many years did a wonderful job at keeping the ship sailing, backed up by many loyal staff members.

George Russell died at the grand old age of 94 in 1951. In that year he figured in the Birthday Honours List, with the award of an M.B.E., he had already received a high honour from the R.H.S. the Veitch Memorial Medal. He was buried in the little churchyard at Boningale, in an unmarked grave, at his own request. There were no flowers, and no fuss at the funeral, he disliked wreaths, and used to say that he would give anyone as many flowers as they liked while they were alive, but none when they were dead! I never met him, but he seems to have had a great twinkle in his eyes in his photographs, and from what I have heard people say he was a very happy man.

Nursery businesses depend very much upon the energy and flair of the people who run them. Jimmy Baker, with his ability and experience became older, and had heart trouble. Some of the men did not come back after the war. New young blood, keen to embrace novel ideas was distrusted, and things gradually began to slide at Baker's Nurseries. Labour became very expensive, gone were the days when there were men at the gate waiting for work. They did not fancy hoeing all day, and the new-fangled weed-killers that were coming in to help the tree and shrub growers were too strong to use on herbaceous subjects. Even the horses were made redundant, to make room for tractors, which needed no attention at the weekends. Pieces of land were sold off, and the sparkle seemed to go from the old nursery business.

An historic picture of three great plantsmen. Left to right: George Russell of lupin fame, Mr Ernest Bishop, who bred the spectacular 'Commonwealth' varieties of delphinium and Mr Watkin Samuel, who was famous for his Red Hot Pokers.

A great mixture of skills is required in horticulture, techniques on the growing side, and the ability to understand and keep up with all the latest advances. Foresight is required, to predict the trends of fashion that are going to be 'in' when the plants are ready to sell in several years' time. It is a labour intensive profession, so management expertise is essential. The game is not yet won even when the plants are grown, they have to be sold, and a whole new set of talents are required to catch the public imagination, and sell the product.

To make matters worse the lupin plants, which had been grown as a monoculture for many years on the same site, developed a virus, which caused stunting of the plant, deformed leaves and general malaise, quickly spreading through the crop. It has since been identified as Cucumber Mosaic Virus, but at the time this was not understood, and rumours abounded that it had been caused by the atom bomb dropped on Hiroshima at the end of the war, or some other retribution for man's wickedness!

By the end of the sixties things certainly looked bad for Baker's Nurseries, and the lupins. In fact even the name was gone, it had been sold off to Bee's, and what remained of Baker's was now known as Boningale Nursery.

Back in 1956, one of the keen young bloods, who arrived at Baker's Nursery straight from college, eager to change the horticultural world, was my husband, Michael Edwards. He took the job of Shrub Foreman at Boningale, and, full of enthusiasm, set to work to rejuvenate the department. One of the innovations he set in motion was one of the first attempts at container growing. He had seen the idea at Bygrave's Nursery in the south, where it had been introduced from America. At that time all orders had to be dispatched during the 'Lifting' season, which for trees and shrubs started in November, and could be quite short. The idea of extending this season by putting the plants into containers seemed a good one, so he approached the local R.A.F. camp and begged all their old tin cans from the cookhouse. It was easy to plant the shrubs into the cans, but there was some difficulty getting them out again, a job, which involved huge pairs of 'tin-snips'. All the 'Old Boys' laughed at the idea, but when Jimmy Baker saw the cash that had been taken during an off season weekend at the site close by the road, he said 'Let the lad have a go at it'. However, Mike found the fight against the old guard very frustrating, and after several years we left Baker's, and started our own business in a very small way in the back garden of our modest 'semi' in the Village.

Nearly 20 years passed, and we prospered, while Baker's declined, until, in 1977, we bought what remained of the fine old Nursery. By then it was reduced to 30 acres or so, with a reasonably modern office, some very decrepit sheds, some glasshouses with scarcely a pane in one piece, a bore hole with access to a good water supply, but a lot of broken irrigation pipes, and a fine crop of weeds. One of the main species of weed was lupins. They grew all over the Nursery, in a rainbow of colours, but varying forms of plants. I remember looking into one of the warehouses, it had stored plastic sacks of lupin seed, but the floor was a jumble of broken glass, chewed up plastic, lupin seeds and rat droppings. Of course we shoveled the lot up into a skip to be dumped, but something made us keep just a couple of jars of the seed, as a memento!

It took a long time, and a lot of hard work to bring the Nursery back into shape. I regret it now, but there was no time to even think about the few lupin plants that were overgrown in the end of a frame. I do not even know whether they were named varieties. We did not have much money to spend on the rescue of the Nursery, so every job had to be carefully costed and planned, and only carried out when we could see our way clear to making things pay.

Chapter 5

NCCPG AND SONNY HEARD TO THE RESCUE!

Eventually things became easier, and by 1985 we had time to enjoy our own 1½-acre garden, which I looked after, having always been a gardener (which is a somewhat different animal to a nurseryman!). At a visit to Chelsea Show I picked up a leaflet from the recently formed National Council for the Conservation of Plants and Gardens. The aim of the Council was to try to preserve plants and gardens, which were in danger of being lost. One of the ideas was to establish a number of Collections of plant types. This was a very clever idea, as it taps the peculiar 'magpie' instinct that so many of us have, to collect things. Once hooked on a collection the owner of that collection inevitably becomes an expert on it, as he or she delves deeper and deeper into the subject.

I joined the steering committee of the newly formed local Shropshire branch of the NCCPG, and we decided to take on a National Collection of *Hamamelis* (witch hazels), winter flowering shrubs, with scented flowers, and quite often excellent autumn tints to the leaves. We extended our garden at Swallow Hayes by another half acre, to make a winter garden in which to house the plants, and of course have had a great deal of fun and interest with it ever since.

As we became involved with the collection of witch hazels it struck us that, with our connection with Baker's Nursery, we really ought to take on a Russell Lupin Collection too. We felt that we owed it to the old man who had given so much of his life to his flowers. To our surprise we found that there had been another 'taker' for the Russell Lupins, Askam Bryan College in Yorkshire, who were close to where George Russell had his original allotments. The collection had been given up after only a short time, which should have warned us that all was not so straightforward as it should have been.

We assumed that we would easily find the original hybrids for our collection in the trade, which was still listing many of the plants. We ordered three of each of as many as we could track down. They duly arrived, and we planted them out. We decided that we would put them in rows, rather than trying to incorporate them into a garden design, as they would be easier to label and keep track of. This turned out to be a good decision in view of the problems that we were about to encounter. These took time to surface, as we had to wait a season first, to see our flowers. To our concern, hardly any of them turned out to be right. We had all the old Baker catalogues, so we knew what they should look like; quite often they were the wrong colour. Sometimes several so called different types were the same. Often the plants showed signs of virus, so we had to eliminate them at once. Out of all the plants we sent off for that first season only six or so turned out to be correct. As our research revealed that Baker's had introduced 152 different named hybrids over the years from 1937 to 1967 this was dreadfully disappointing.

Our next tack was to try to find the original plants remaining in gardens. A couple were discovered in gardens in the village, where people had kept them going for nostalgic reasons. An article in the *Sunday Times* by Francesca Greenoak asking for information on any original Russell hybrids did not turn up a single plant, although I had plenty of letters showing interest in our project. The problem with maintaining the strain of the Russell Lupin is compounded by the fact that it contains annual genes, probably from the annual species *Lupinus luteus*, which George Russell had to use in order to get the colour yellow fixed in the strain. Further to this is the fact that lupins self seed very readily, often a seedling plant growing in the centre of an existing plant, giving rise to the myth that the plants 'revert'. This just not true, it is a new seedling that has taken the place of the original plant.

At this point, feeling very disappointed, we decided that we would continue to look for original hybrids, but not very hopefully. In addition we would start to grow our own seed, and select again from that, in the same way that George Russell had, so many years ago. After all, we had a very good start, as we had the rescued seed from the dilapidated warehouse, and also the Nursery at Boningale still sprouted a large range of seedling weeds. Accordingly, we collected seed from the best of the weeds, and sowed that, together with the "rescue" seed, and grew on 300 plants, ready to plant out. We also dug up the best of the 'weeds', and planted them in the garden at Swallow Hayes, to strengthen our new strain, trying to get a good range of colours.

I contacted the NCCPG, to see if we could still claim to hold a National Collection of Russell Lupins. They replied in the affirmative. National Collections were there to save plants that would otherwise be lost, so that was exactly what we were trying to do, even if the original Russell hybrids had disappeared.

Now a further blow struck, my husband died in July 1986. My children, who had been trained in horticulture, but had little experience, took over the running of the Nursery. Our staff were wonderful, backing up our efforts at recovery, but of course extra projects, such as the lupins had to take a back seat.

Eventually, when we had more time to consider, I planted out our potted seedlings into the garden. They turned out to be fairly good, which cheered me up; it is best to be busy in such circumstances, so I went to see Arthur Heard, who was living in the village, and asked his advice on my little crop. He was very critical, and we got rid of more than three quarters of the plants, but he kindly started to teach me the points of a good Russell Lupin. All the 'spaced out' spikes, showing stem behind the florets had to go, as well as the plants that split up and fell over. Any with the standards squeezed so that they did not cover the stem were banished, we called those 'pinched standards'. Also any with the standard petal crowded round the bell were disapproved of, even though I thought they looked quite good. These we christened 'hooded standards'. Sometimes the 'bell' was inclined to split, these were thrown out. To my disappointment Arthur frowned on all the blue ones, which I thought were rather pretty, they were got rid of along with any murky colours that I might have considered quite arty. We marked just a few to take seed from, and I labeled them carefully, using the prefix A, to denote that they were seedlings from 1986. B would be for 1987, and so on.

In 1988 I planted out 5,000 seedlings in the field next to the garden. Arthur came up when they came into flower, and together we got rid of 4,800 of them! The next year, after a trial period we were left with only about 20 plants that we thought were reasonable. This proportion of 'good' seedlings is about average I have found, one per 250 seedlings, though they do improve, as the selections get better.

I found also that it was very necessary to trial the seedlings for several years, as some of them would turn out to be annual types. It is so frustrating to find that a beautiful seedling turns up, perfect in all respects, but then drops dead in the winter because it is an annual! This, of course reflects the fact that George Russell did use annual strains, which fortunately seem to be a recessive trait, amongst his original seed, to get the full rainbow of colours.

In order to keep the virus at bay I had to be very sure that no sucking insects, such as aphis, attacked the plants, as virus is spread by the action of the sucking. To my horror, a really virulent strain of aphis appeared, huge horrible greyish insects, arrived on the plants, reducing the spikes to a sodden mass, seemingly overnight. They had come in from America, and lived in the roots over winter, a spate of mild winters in the early 90's allowed them to multiply, and I found I had to spray the plants very regularly with a systemic insecticide to keep them clear. They were just too fecund for my ladybirds to cope with.

By the early 90's I had a reasonable selection of varieties that Arthur Heard reckoned were good, a few he even admitted were very good! So I began to multiply the best of my seedlings by the old method of taking cuttings or dividing the plants in early spring. However, I realised that this method would be too labour intensive to use if I ever managed to produce enough really good selections to offer to the public. Also, any virus present is multiplied with the cuttings, so I looked into the use of micropropagation to produce a large quantity of plants suitable to sell.

This method involves a tiny piece of the growing tip, or meristem, of the plant being grown in a test tube, eventually to emerge as a tiny plantlet that is potted on. Quite a

John Snocken working with the lupin propagation at Ashwoods Nursery, seen here with some of the selections in 2003.

Some of the new lupin hybrid selected plants that have been named, and will be on the market soon.

Bo-Peep *is a direct descendant of the original* George Russell.

Mary, Mary Quite Contrary *is to join* Tom, Tom *on the market next Autumn.*

Wicked Witch *(left) makes a contrast with the pure white* Snow White *(right).*

Peter Piper *was picked out of the weeds at Boningale back in 1985, he is very reliable.*

This blue and white bi-colour is to be named Tom, Tom the Piper's Son.

Knave of Hearts *is a strong cultivar.*

Simple Simon *is a beautiful clear yellow.*

One of the 2003 seedlings which has been selected for trial.

bit of research is required before the various gels and formulae are suitable. One of the advantages is that it is possible to clean up any diseases at the same time. I had a small batch of plants propagated by this method, and worked out the timing to produce saleable plants.

My first choice of a company to produce and promote the plants was unfortunate, as they went bankrupt soon after accepting my plants, which wasted several years. It took time to recover my confidence. I had continued to select the best plants, though I missed Arthur Heard, who had sadly died. Arthur had taught me a great deal, so the thread of experience was not broken; through him I had received, almost directly, instruction from George Russell himself, even though I never actually met him.

The next step was to find a nurseryman with the ability to propagate and promote the selections. I found the answer nearby, at Ashwood Nursery, with John Massey at the helm. At Ashwood enthusiasm flourishes, backed up by excellent basic horticultural practices and knowledge. In the capable hands of his team, Philip Baulk in charge of trial management, and John Snocken at the practical end, my cuttings have flourished, a micro propagation laboratory has been located, and, hopefully, the Russell Lupins will soon be on the market again.

We now have seedlings from the very best plants growing both here at Swallow Hayes and also at Ashwood, where they have delighted us with the quality compared to my original 5,000 in 1988. We have actually named the first batch of selections, and hope to offer them to the public by 2004. Choosing names for ones 'babies' is exciting. Like real babies they almost seem to name themselves. The really wicked looking A10 just had to be 'Wicked Witch', and then the pure white M10 was obviously 'Snow White'. To accompany them the pretty C65, with pink bells and white standards is 'Bo Peep', while the large yellow L5 cried out to be 'Simple Simon'. The very reliable A26, originally picked out by my husband Mike from the weeds at Boningale in 1985 is pumpkin coloured, so 'Peter Piper, Pumpkin Eater' seemed to suit. C38 is cerise, with a white flash on the standard – just right for the 'Knave of Hearts'. There are many others coming along, each so different, yet perfect companions for each other and other herbaceous plants or shrubs.

The excitement of seeing the new plants coming into flower for the first time never ceases to thrill. The longer I watch the plants the more I appreciate the patience and skill of George Russell, who had the dream and the ability to make it come true. Russell Hybrids are some of the best paints in the gardener's palette, it will be wonderful to see them being used once again.

Chapter 6

THE FUTURE

Since George Russell's time there have been a number of attempts to establish further strains from the original Russell hybrids. Several seed houses have produced seed that come fairly reliably true to colour. The Gallery strain, bred in France, which comes more or less true to colour and the Band of Nobles, which also comes true to type are available, but the form of the spikes and plants sometimes are not so good. George Russell himself did start to breed a strain of dwarf lupins, more suited to smaller gardens, or windy sites. The seed strain Lulu is based on this premise. Thompson and Morgan have introduced a Russell derived dwarf seed strain called Tutti Fruttii. I would like to select dwarf types to expand our own range, as quite often a small variety does occur amongst the selections.

John Walker, a retired policeman, has grown lupins from seed that Arthur Heard gave him many years ago, and produced some fine types. The Woodfield brothers, Maurice and Brian, have been hybridizing stock for many years, also helped at first by Arthur Heard, at their nursery near Stratford on Avon. They have shown magnificent plants at Chelsea on a number of occasions, so have kept up the interest in these wonderful plants. In the West Country Sarah Conibear has been offering her selections to the public for several years. She has produced some fine varieties from seed that she acquired of the original Russell strain. I remember sending her some seed way back in 1997!

The Russell Hybrid Lupins are the stalwarts of early summer, giving height and vertical lines to borders, in addition to the wonderful range of colours, which can bring designs to life. Many people remember the scent of lupins on a sunny day with great nostalgia from childhood, when the sense of smell is superior, and the spikes of blossom may well have been over their heads!

A vase or bowl of lupins can look really spectacular. As the growth is fairly soft, and the stems hollow it is best to strip the foliage off, then tip them up and fill the stems with water before standing them in a deep amount of water. They will grow towards the light, or upwards, so if they are to remain straight they will need to be stood upright. There is a story about George Russell's first trip to the York Gala Show. He carried them very carefully in long boxes held horizontally, but when he opened the boxes at the show they had all turned up at the ends, so looked ridiculous when placed in their vases.

Lupins are easy to cultivate, they like a well-drained, open sunny position or partial shade. They do not need a particularly fertile soil, as they manufacture their own nitrogen through the leguminous nodules on their roots. The ground should ideally be on the acid side, as they do not like a limey soil. They dislike being too dry; hoeing around the plants will help to conserve moisture as well as reducing competition from weeds. In very dry spring weather they will appreciate some irrigation to sustain the developing flower heads. To really spoil them a dressing of bone meal or a seaweed fertilizer, which contains various trace elements in it is beneficial. Manure is to be avoided, as it may cause rotting. Nitrogen in any form is not good as it would encourage lush leaf growth, and weaken the stems. This makes the plants vulnerable to wind damage, and also more susceptible to rotting in the winter months.

Thinning of the flower spikes before they bloom to five to seven spikes will ensure that the plant can support quality blossoms. Each seedling is different, and some will flower early in the season in late May, the majority come in the first week in June as a rule, but some may be later. If the flowering heads are removed after flowering this will prevent seeding, and the plant may produce more flowers towards the autumn. The ability to do this does vary with the variety, so it may be a good idea to plant a late flowering plant in front of the lupins, to ensure a succession of flowers in the border. If the cultivation is kept up the foliage by itself, with the lush palmate leaves, can be very attractive.

The presence of annual species in the original strain does mean that the plants are fairly short lived. If they are divided regularly, or reproduced from cuttings, this helps to prolong the life expectancy of good plants.

Because the plants produce their own nitrogen they are sometimes used as a green manure crop. A crop of an annual, such as *Lupinus angustifolius* or *Lupinus luteus* is sown, to be ploughed under at the end of the year, thus enriching the soil with nitrogen. Do not let garden lupins be cross- pollinated by these types, as annual traits will then become more evident!

The easiest way to increase good plants is to divide them in early spring, as they start to grow. A sharp spade is used to cut the root cleanly, making sure there are shoots on each piece. It is important to make sure there is some fibrous root present. Often it is possible to cut off an 'Irishman's cutting', being a shoot which has grown sideways, so has some roots attached to it.

The best time to take cuttings is when the plants start into growth after the winter. This can be from the end of January to March, depending on the weather. A sharp knife is used to slice off a new shoot, with a piece of the hard, yellow coloured rootstock attached to it. Any superfluous foliage is cut off cleanly, as this could lead to rotting. The cutting is then potted into a small pot of fairly gritty compost, kept moist and protected from the worst of the weather by a cold frame or greenhouse, kept cool, and with no direct sunshine. They will root in a matter of a few weeks. It is also possible to take soft cuttings from the axils of the leaves in summer, but these tend to be very soft, and need much more care to root successfully.

Lupins are not difficult to grow from seed, although the outer skin of the seed is tough, so they are usually nicked with a sharp knife and sometimes also soaked for 24 hours or so before sowing to enable moisture to enter the seed. They have been known to germinate after a very long time, fortunate for the seed that we found in the derelict warehouse! We found delphinium seed at the same time, from the famous 'Commonwealth' strain, raised by Ernest Bishop. They were actually in airtight kilner jars, but none of them were viable when the jars were opened and sown by the Delphinium Society, to whom I gave them.

Lupins can be sown from February onwards in ordinary compost in deep boxes, so that the taproot can go down. They should be transplanted to their flowering positions from June to August; at this stage the nitrogen nodules can be plainly seen. They should flower either during that autumn, when it is probably advisable to cut off the flower heads, or the following spring. Alternatively they can be sown in a cold greenhouse or frame in September, to be potted on as they grow, and should flower the following May or June. Another option is that they can be sown under glass in February of March, and should be flowering the following summer.

Modern hybridists 'cross' two chosen parents in an artificial way. This is done by emasculating the flowers, that is cutting off the stamens or pollen producing parts of the chosen mother flowers, so that they cannot pollinate themselves. Then the flower head is 'bagged', by tying a paper bag over it so that no pollen from another plant can reach it. Next the pollen from the chosen father plant is introduced on a paintbrush, thus ensuring that the father and mother of the resulting seedling are chosen for certain characteristics.

Pests and diseases to which lupins are prone have tended to give them a bad name in recent years, but most of these can be controlled.

The dreaded lupin aphis (*Macrosiphum albifrons*) arrived from America in 1981, when it was discovered at Kew. It spread rapidly from there, and was being found in Scotland within three years, and is now also in Europe. It has no alternative host but lupins, so spends the entire year on these plants. It overwinters on the basal buds, cosily protected from the cold weather, and begins building up again during spring and early summer. Populations of this large, grey-green aphis usually reach a peak just as the lupins are coming into flower when infestations can become so heavy that the plant collapses. During the summer winged forms develop, and these fly off to find new lupins to infest. Possibly because it is not native to this country the usual aphis predators and parasites seem to have little interest in this pest. It needs to be controlled before a damaging attack has developed. As soon as the insects are detected a suitable insecticide, such as the contact spray bifenthrin or systemic insectide imidacloprid could be used. Organic gardeners may prefer a product based on natural materials such as pyrethrum. Whatever insecticide is used it should be avoided while the flowers are open if possible, to avoid harming bees or other pollinating insects. If it is necessary to spray during the flowering season this should be done in the evening when bees are less likely to be visiting the flowers.

Slugs and snails find the lupin foliage tasty as it matures. More damaging to the plants is the small, keel shaped slug that burrows into the soil around the roots during cold spells and can weaken the plant in early spring. Slug pellets or a liquid formulation based on formaldehyde can be used to deter these pests.

Virus, causing disfiguring symptoms, such as mottling or curling of the leaves, occasionally affects plants. It is best to remove and destroy these plants.

Various lupin spots, caused by fungus infections sometimes cause brown lesions to appear on the young leaves, petioles and stems, leading to wilting and dieback. They can be successfully treated with Bordeaux powder after cutting back the affected foliage.

Powdery mildew sometimes occurs late in the season as a greyish white powdery coating. It is more likely to happen if plants are stressed by dry soil conditions. The affected areas can be removed if it is very unsightly.

The best way to avoid fungal or bacterial problems is to grow the plants well, and not allow them to get too dry. A mulch of organic matter can help to alleviate draught conditions.

Fasciation is quite common in lupins. The flower spike becomes flattened and distorted. This may be caused by weed killer, but can occur without any apparent reason in a number of plants. If the fascinated flower spikes are cut off the plant usually recovers and grows normally again.

The future of the Russell Lupin strain lies with gardeners and nurserymen who care about it. If the plants are left to themselves they will take the easy way, which means that the strongest genes in the plants will overpower the weaker, recessive genes, and inevitably the strain will gradually recede into the drabber colours and poorer spikes of the species that George Russell used to produce the strain. It is amazingly strong, as is shown by the naturalized groups of plants that grow alongside railway banks or in parts of New Zealand where it has escaped from gardens to colonise, but in order to keep it a selection process has to continue.

Even as far back as 1939 it was realized how fragile was the strain. *Amateur Gardening* of June 1939 ran a long article by 'Domarin'. It pointed out the dangers of the widespread growing of Russell Lupins in gardens, where some amateur growers did not understand the importance of selecting the best only.

Everybody has a part to play. If good points of the Russell strain are understood and encouraged, by vegetative propagation or selection of seeds from the best plants, just as George Russell did, and 'bad' plants are not allowed to grow the strain could actually improve. It is a challenge for every gardener!

References

Readers Digest Encyclopedia of Plants and Flowers, 1978.
Sanders Encyclopedia of Gardening, 1952.
My Garden Book by John Weathers, 1924.
Gardeners Assistant by Robert Thompson, 1886.
English Flower Garden by William Robinson, 1903.
Perennial Garden Plants by Graham Stuart Thomas, 1990.
The Russell Lupin by Ronald Parrett, 1959.
R.H.S. Journal, 1966.
A-Z Encyclopedia Garden Plants edited by Christopher Brickell, 1996.
Baker's Nursery catalogues from 1906 on.

Postscript

Ashwood Nursery is to offer genuine Russell Lupin strain seed for sowing in the Spring of 2004. Named varieties from cuttings should be on sale by Autumn 2004.

RUSSELL LUPINS
Mixed Hybrids
(Flowering June)
Height $3\frac{1}{2}$ ft.

Soil: preferably light soil, but any type is suitable except one with excessive lime. Plant in open sunny position. **Preparation:** no humus in any form of peat or manure should be used. Bonemeal at 4 oz. to the square yard is recommended. **Planting:** soak plant and pot for 15 minutes, remove pot and plant 18 in. apart with crown of plant just above soil level. Firm thoroughly. **Aftercare:** repeat dressing of Bonemeal in Spring every 2nd year (annually on poor ground). Remove dead flower spikes immediately.

GOOD GARDENING SERIES

The original cards that were sold with the first Russell Lupin seeds.

Available from:
Ashwood Nurseries Limited
Ashwood Lower Lane
Kingswinford
West Midlands, DY6 0AE
England

Boningale as it is today.